Great Houses and G... of Dorset

by Robert Westwood

Inspiring Places Publishing
2 Down Lodge Close
Alderholt
Fordingbridge
SP6 3JA
inspiringplaces.co.uk

ISBN 978-0-9928073-8-2

Contains Ordnance Survey data © Crown copyright and database right (2011)

Contents

3   Introduction

4   Minterne House

6   Mapperton

9   Sherborne Castle

12   Abbotsbury Sub-tropical Gardens

14   Athelhampton House

16   Shaftesbury Abbey

18   Kingston Lacy

20   Hardy's Cottage

22   Edmondsham House

24   Sandford Orcas Manor

26   Larmer Tree Gardens

28   Compton Acres

30   Knoll Gardens

32   Kingston Maurward

34   Bennett's Water Gardens

36   Forde Abbey

39   Map of Locations

40   Acknowledgements and Notes

Left: Sherborne Castle gardens in autumn. (Jayson Hutchins)

Introduction

Dorset's beautiful rural landscape is still home to many country estates, some with grand mansions at their heart others with more modest but charming manor houses. A number were carved from the extensive lands once owned by prosperous abbeys and monasteries following the Dissolution under Henry VIII. Some remain private and mostly hidden, but many are open to the public providing an enjoyable and relaxing day out in a glorious setting. Fashions changed in the eighteenth century and landowners began to develop and appreciate a more natural style of parkland rather than formal gardens. Sweeping, gently undulating meadows, clumps of trees and serpentine lakes characterised the parklands of grand houses, many designed by Lancelot 'Capability' Brown. Some wealthy landowners were keen horticulturalists themselves and brought back hundreds of plant species from their travels all over the world. These activities have left Dorset with a rich heritage of landscape gardens that provide the perfect setting for its grand houses.

This book seeks to provide a guide to Dorset's great houses and gardens that are open to the public with colour illustrations hopefully giving some idea of the delights that await the visitor. Practical details are included and a brief history of each location; many have fascinating stories. Some are open all year, others for just a day or two each week in the summer. A few locations are simply gardens with no great house to explore, but all will provide a great day out. *NB - Opening times and prices are correct at the time of writing, please check before you visit.*

Minterne House

On A352 between Sherborne and Dorchester, DT2 7AU
minterne.co.uk

In 1660 Minterne House was leased to the first Sir Winston Churchill, ancestor of his later famous namesake. His son, General Charles Churchill, a veteran of the Battle of Blenheim where he fought with his brother the Duke of Marlborough, lived at Minterne from 1688 to 1714 and made considerable improvements to the house and gardens. In 1768 the estate was bought by Admiral Robert Digby, younger brother of Lord Digby of Sherborne Castle, and it has remained in the hands of the Digby family ever since. Robert Digby found the valley rather barren and set about landscaping it, in particular using the River Cerne to create lakes and cascades and planting many trees. The parkland at Sherborne was, at this time, being altered to the designs of Capability Brown and Robert travelled over there on several occasions to ask the advice of the great landscape gardener. Robert also started the collection of azaleas and rhododendrons; this was greatly enhanced in the late nineteenth and early twentieth centuries by the tenth Lord Digby. During this time many new species of plants were brought back to England from the Himalayas, China and Japan by explorers sponsored by wealthy landowners. Between 1902 and 1907 Lord Digby also had Minterne House completely rebuilt using Ham Stone, a local, golden Jurassic limestone. Today the house is still in private hands and is not open to visitors. However, the wonderful landscaped gardens are open and, as might be expected, are a particular delight in spring when the azaleas and rhododendrons are in bloom. There are also wonderful colours in autumn.

Open: Daily 10am to 6pm, 13 February - 9 November. Adults £5, children free, dogs on leads welcome. Free parking opposite church.

Far left: Minterne House. Pictures left and opposite: Early summer in the gardens.

Mapperton

2 miles from Beaminster on B3163, DT8 3NR
mapperton.com

Tucked away in rolling countryside north of the little market town of Beaminster, Mapperton House offers the visitor a real sense of having discovered a timeless rural treasure. The small Jacobean manor house has some features from the Tudor period but was largely rebuilt in the 1660s. There was a manor here when the Domesday Book was compiled and throughout its history has been owned by several wealthy families. The village it was the heart of never recovered from the plague of 1666 and now has relatively few residents. The manor was bought by Victor Montagu in 1955 and today is held by his son the Earl of Sandwich.

The wonderful and unusual Italianate gardens were laid out in the 1920s by the then owner Ethel Labouchere and sit in a sheltered valley behind the manor. The topiary, ornamental sculptures, ponds, fountains and extensive collection of shrubs and trees help make it an unforgettable experience.

Such a lovely and atmospheric location as this has inevitably been used as a film location a number of times, and in 2015 was Bathsheba Everdene's farmhouse in Thomas Hardy's *Far from the Madding Crowd*.

Open: Gardens, 1 March - 31 October, 11am to 5pm every day except Saturday. House, 2 April March - 31 October, 12pm to 4pm every day except Friday and Saturday, guided tours only. Adults house and garden £12, garden only £9, under 16 free. Dogs are not allowed in house or gardens.
Pictures left and pages 7 and 8 show the house and gardens.

Sherborne Castle

In Sherborne, DT9 5NR
sherbornecastle.com

Confusingly, there are two Sherborne Castles, an "old" one and a "new" one. Old Sherborne Castle, now just ruins, was built for Roger of Caen, Bishop of Salisbury in the twelfth century. As Chancellor to Henry I he accumulated vast wealth. During the civil war between King Stephen and the Empress Matilda the castle was besieged and taken by the king. A legend tells of a curse made by the first Bishop of Salisbury that promised misfortune to any layman who held land belonging to the bishopric. This seems to have been the case for the castle until King Edward III handed it back to the church.

New Sherborne Castle was the creation of the famous Elizabethan adventurer Sir Walter Raleigh. He had fallen in love with the setting of the old castle and persuaded Queen Elizabeth to grant him the lease. However, he found it impractical as a home; so in 1594 he had the new castle built. After Sir Walter's fall from grace (was it the curse again?) it was acquired by the diplomat Sir John Digby and has been in the hands of the Digby family since 1617. Sir John added four wings to Walter Raleigh's simple rectangular design and, apart from an extension in 1787, the house has changed little since.

In 1753 'Capability' Brown was given one of his first commissions at Sherborne and the beautiful parkland we see today is largely the result of his inspiration. He created the fifty acre lake and planted many specimen trees and herbaceous borders. There are around forty two acres of this Grade 1 listed garden to explore, with views over many more acres of lovely parkland.

Open: 1 April - 29 October, closed Monday and Friday, open bank holidays and Good Friday. Gardens 10am to 6pm, castle 11am to 5pm. Adults garden only £6.50, castle and garden £12, under 16 free. Dogs are welcome in the gardens. Pictures left and pages 10 and 11 show the castle and gardens.

Abbotsbury Sub-tropical Gardens

In Abbotsbury, DT3 4LA
abbotsbury-tourism.co.uk

The extensive lands of Abbotsbury Abbey were leased to Sir Giles Strangways in 1541 after the Dissolution of the Monasteries and have been held by his descendants ever since. Today much of Abbotsbury, including the gardens, are owned by the Ilchester Estate. Stephen Fox, MP for Shaftesbury and Privy Counsellor, was created 1st Earl of Ilchester in 1756; he had married into the Strangways family in 1735 and later added their name to his own. In 1765 the daughter of the first earl's mother-in-law, Elizabeth, became 1st Countess of Ilchester. The family's main home was Melbury House but the Countess had a summer residence built at Abbotsbury overlooking the Fleet. A walled kitchen garden was created a short distance away and gradually expanded. The 4th Earl of Ilchester was a foreign diplomat and also an expert botanist and plant collector; he introduced many new species to the garden and with the continued interest and attention of his successors it became one of the finest in England and home to thousands of species from all over the world. Sadly the summer residence, Abbotsbury Castle, burnt down in 1913 but despite a period of neglect between the two world wars the gardens are once more a glorious spectacle. New species have been added from all over the world and there is colour all year round.

Open: Every day except 19 December - 2 January inclusive.
10am to 5pm or 4pm in winter.
Adults £12, children 5-15 £9.
Dogs welcome. Discount for advanced booking
Pictures left and opposite page show the luxuriant gardens in late summer.

Athelhampton House

Near Puddletown off A35, DT2 7LG
athelhampton.co.uk

The homely manor of Athelhampton has been privately owned throughout its history. In Saxon times an estate here was held by a man called Aethelric, from whom the present name was derived, but in the Domesday Book of 1086 it was known as "Pidele" after the river (now Piddle) which flows by the side of the house. During the fourteenth century the manor came into the hands of the Martyn family. In 1485 Sir William Martyn had the Great Hall built and it remains a fine example of Tudor architecture. Sir William was a successful politician and in 1492 became the Lord Mayor of London. His tomb is in the nearby church at Puddletown.

Athelhampton remained with the Martyn family for four generations, but after they failed to produce any male heirs it passed through a succession of different owners. By the late nineteenth century the estate was in quite a run down condition until it was acquired by Alfred de Lafontaine who set about restoring the house and creating the now spectacular gardens. In 1957 the house was bought by Robert Cooke who gave it to his son Sir Robert Cooke, MP in 1966 – it remains with the Cooke family today. Part of the charm of Athelhampton is that the family are very much involved in the day to day running and maintenance of the house and garden; its upkeep is a real labour of love, involving many local people too.

Open: March - October, Sundays to Thursdays 10:30am to 5pm. Closed Friday and Saturday.
November - February, Sundays only 10:30am to dusk.
Adults £13.50, under 16 £3.00, dogs on leads £1.00. Gardens only £9.50.

Left: The gardens, and opposite page: The lovely west wing of the house.

Shaftesbury Abbey

Park Walk in Shaftesbury, SP7 8JR
shaftesburyabbey.org.uk

Shaftesbury was once an important, thriving town. It was established by Alfred the Great, one of a number of fortified "burghs" designed as places of refuge in the event of Viking attacks. Only foundations now remain of the once prosperous abbey founded in 888 AD by King Alfred who installed his daughter Aethelgifu as the first abbess. Its wealth and fame grew after it had become the resting place for the body of King Edward the Martyr who was murdered at Corfe Castle in 978 AD, possibly on the orders of his step-mother Aelfthryth who wanted her son Ethelred to be king. The body was originally buried in Wareham but later transferred to Shaftesbury with great ceremony. Tales of miracles surrounding the body soon started circulating and in 1001 Edward was recognised as a saint, ensuring the prosperity of the abbey for five hundred years as a place of pilgrimage. Remains thought to be Edward's were uncovered in 1931

and following a long dispute were reburied in an Eastern Orthodox church near Woking where Edward is still regarded as a saint. A modern shrine at Shaftesbury marks the spot of Edward's grave there.

A charming, intimate garden has been planted in and around the foundations of the abbey. This includes a medieval orchard and a herb garden, both featuring plants, fruits and herbs that would have been used by the nuns. The Dissolution of the Monasteries in 1539 saw the abbey closed after more than six hundred years of continual worship. Outside the abbey is a lovely terrace with gardens overlooking the Vale of Blackmore. The view across this fertile vale is extensive, and all of it once belonged to the abbey.

Open: Daily from 21 March - 31 October, 10am to 5pm.
Adults £3, under 17 free.
Left: The statue of King Alfred and a stained glass window commemorating King Edward the Martyr.
Opposite: The abbey garden.

Kingston Lacy

West of Wimborne on B3082, BH21 4EA
nationaltrust.org.uk/kingstonlacy

In the seventeenth century the wealthy Bankes family owned two Dorset estates. Their main residence was Corfe Castle but they also held extensive lands around Wimborne. The family were staunch Royalists and after the famous siege of Corfe Castle where the gallant Lady Mary Bankes led the defenders, the castle was slighted on the orders of Parliament. The fortunes of the family rose again with the restoration of the monarchy and they regained their estates. Rather than rebuild Corfe Castle they chose to build a new house on their other estate near Wimborne, which was completed in 1665. Known as Kingston Hall, it was a red brick structure and was home to the Bankes family until 1981 when Ralph Bankes bequeathed the estate to the National Trust. In the nineteenth century William John Bankes had had the house faced with limestone and changed the name to Kingston Lacy. Over the years the family acquired an impressive collection of paintings and fine art, including works by Titian, Velazquez, Van Dyck and Brueghel. Also on display is the world's largest individual collection of Egyptian antiques.

The house is surrounded by around three hundred acres of parkland and formal gardens, so there is much to explore. A seven acre Japanese garden and a walled Victorian kitchen garden are among the highlights.

Open: House, 1 March - 30 October, 11am to 5pm. 31 October - 31 December, 11am to 4pm. Gardens all year, 1 March - 30 October, 11am to 6pm, rest of year 11am to 4pm.
Adult, house £13.50, child £6.70, garden and park adult £8.60, child £4.30. Dogs welcome in park. Pictures left and opposite: House and gardens.

Hardy's Cottage

Higher Bockhampton near Dorchester, DT2 8QJ
nationaltrust.org.uk/hardys-cottage

Anyone who has read and enjoyed Thomas Hardy's descriptions of Wessex in his novels will not be disappointed to find he was born and raised in such an idyllic and peaceful setting; but one where the hardships of life in nineteenth century rural England are as apparent as the natural beauty. Hardy's cottage in Higher Bockhampton near Dorchester, is a traditional cob and thatch construction, built in 1800 by his great grandfather. It was here that Thomas Hardy was born in 1840 and lived until he was thirty-four when he married Emma Gifford. The house has been little altered since it was built and the furniture inside is from the period, although not the original owned by the Hardy family. Two of Hardy's great Wessex novels were written here, *Under the Greenwood Tree* in 1872 and *Far from the Madding Crowd* in 1874. In front of the cottage is a delightful cottage garden. Such gardens were originally intended to produce food and later also became places to enjoy with informal plantings of flowers amongst the fruit and vegetables. They provided a charming contrast to the formal gardens popular with the owners of large country houses.

    Under the Greenwood Tree was Hardy's second published novel and was set around Higher Bockhampton, renamed 'Mellstock' in the book. Central to the story is the church choir, based on the nearby Stinsford Church where

Hardy's heart and several relatives lie buried. You may also want to visit Max Gate, the home Hardy designed himself and where he lived from 1885 until his death in 1928. Only three miles from Hardy's Cottage and within walking distance of Dorchester, this is where Hardy wrote most of his poetry and his two most controversial novels, *Tess of the D'Urbervilles* and *Jude the Obscure.*

Open: 9 March - 30 October, Wednesday to Sunday, 11am to 5pm. Adult £6, child £3. Dogs welcome in garden and surrounding woodland. Cottage is 15 minute walk from car park where there is a visitor centre and cafe.
Pictures left and opposite: Hardy's cottage and garden.

Edmondsham House

North of Wimborne off B3078, BH21 5RE

There has been a manor here since Saxon times, and once belonged to Queen Matilda, wife of William the Conqueror. The story of how it came to belong to Matilda is an unusual and sad one. While a young princess, Matilda is said to have become infatuated with a Saxon ambassador in Lille named Brihtric, who was lord of the estates around Cranborne. He rejected her advances and she took revenge after the Conquest, having him thrown into prison and his lands confiscated. The present house, apart from a Georgian extension, dates from Tudor times and has been held by the same family since the sixteenth century. It is surrounded by six acres of lovely gardens with many mature trees and shaped hedges, and a productive Victorian walled garden with colourful herbaceous borders and vegetable plots. When the house is open, a tour is given by the owner, a charming experience matched by the owner of Sandford Orcas manor. Don't be surprised if the two recommend each other, they are brother and sister! Nearby is Castle Hill, also owned by the Edmondsham Estate, where you can wander around the remains of the Norman motte and bailey castle. The castle was a wooden structure so no buildings remain, but it is a beautiful spot, particularly in spring when the ground is covered with bluebells. Cranborne Manor is a near neighbour and it is possible to visit the garden there on the same day, conveniently, they are both open (gardens only) on Wednesday afternoons in summer.

Open: House and garden, Bank Holiday Mondays, Wednesdays in April and October only, 2pm to 5pm.
Garden, April - October inclusive, Wednesdays and Sundays 2pm to 5pm. Small fee, no dogs allowed.
Pictures left: The walled garden.
Opposite: The house.

Sandford Orcas Manor

In Sandford Orcas, north of Sherborne, DT9 4SB

Sandford Orcas is a tiny village three miles north of Sherborne, very close to the boundary with Somerset. Many of the buildings there, including the charming manor house, are built with the local Ham Hill Stone, a golden, Jurassic limestone also used to build Sherborne Abbey. The second part of the name derives from the Norman lord of the manor and it is assumed that the present house, dating from around 1550, was built on the site of his house. The manor is largely unaltered, apart from some surprisingly careful Victorian restoration, and is surely one of the best preserved Tudor manors in the whole of the country. The relatively small garden is lovely with mature herbaceous borders and neat lawns.

In 1736 the house was bought by a local lawyer named Hutchings and his descendants have owned it ever since. The present owner, Sir Mervyn Medlycott, has also been responsible for some expert restoration and personally conducts visitors on a tour of the house during opening times. The house came to Sir Mervyn in 1978 and had been previously let to a retired soldier, Colonel Francis Claridge. Colonel Claridge opened the house to the public, and although not initially a huge success, the emergence of more and more lurid ghost stories generated greater public interest. So much so that Sandford Orcas has been called by some the most haunted house in England. The owner is sceptical, and feels, as many do, that the sudden proliferation of ghostly sightings by the Colonel and his family was suspiciously coincidental and convenient.

Open: May - September, Monday and Sunday, 2pm to 5pm. (closed in June) Adult £5, child £2.50.

Pictures left and opposite: The manor and garden.

Larmer Tree Gardens

Tollard Royal, off A354, SP5 5PY
larmertree.co.uk

Now well known for its successful summer and autumn festivals, at other times the Larmer Tree Gardens offer visitors a chance to relax and unwind in an enchanting, tranquil setting. Right on the border of Dorset and Wiltshire, the origin of the name is obscure. It was originally spelt 'Lavermere', 'mere' meaning some sort of boundary. The area was a popular hunting location for King John who is said to have met with huntsmen under the branches of the Larmer Tree, probably a Wych elm that was still alive as late as 1894. In 1999 a new Larmer Tree was planted to mark the Millennium.

The gardens are part of the Rushmore Estate, inherited in 1880 by General Augustus Lane Fox (later changed to Pitt Rivers). It was he who created the gardens for public entertainment, enjoyment and education; the first privately owned gardens to be open to the public. Each year thousands came to relax, picnic and listen to the entertainments. Buildings were erected around the gardens and at night thousands of Vauxhall lights provided illumination for dancing on the lawns. Sadly the gardens closed in 1900 after the death of Pitt Rivers and remained neglected until 1991 when the general's great grandson Michael Pitt Rivers began their renovation, opening them again in 1995.

We have another reason to be grateful to General Pitt Rivers; the Rushmore Estate covered 27 000 acres of Cranborne Chase, around which were scattered hundreds of Bronze Age burial mounds and other ancient sites. Pitt Rivers organised their systematic excavation, recording and preserving the finds for future generations. He was, perhaps, the first scientific archaeologist.

Open: 26 March - 31 October, Sunday to Thursday 11am to 4:30pm. Also closed for festivals and special events - check website for details or telephone 01725 516971. Dogs not allowed except in cafe garden.
Adult £4, child £2.50, under 5 free.
Left: The gardens.
Opposite: The main lawn and stage.

Compton Acres

Canford Cliffs Road, Poole, BH13 7ES
comptonacres.co.uk

Compton Acres offers the visitor ten acres of luxuriant and varied gardens to explore with over three thousand species of trees and plants from all over the world. Poole may seem an odd location for such an attraction; after all, up until the beginning of the nineteenth century much of what is now Poole and Bournemouth was a barren heathland. To create such a feature in the 1920s from a sparsely wooded heath was no mean feat and was largely due to the vision of one man, Thomas William Simpson. Simpson was a local entrepreneur who had made a fortune manufacturing margarine and had developed a passionate interest in plants during his travels all over the world. He employed a team who moved thousands of tons of rocks and earth to landscape the gardens and reputedly spent £220 000, many millions by today's prices. The gardens were developed around an existing large house but it is thought that they were always intended to be open to the public and not just a private paradise.

Although understandably neglected during World War II, the gardens reopened in 1952. Thomas Simpson died in 1944 and since then there have been a number of owners, all of whom have continued to develop the site. Today Compton Acres features formal gardens, including Italian, Japanese, heather and rock and water gardens, as well as woodland areas. The Japanese garden is regarded as one of the finest in Britain. This variety ensures that, whatever the time of year you visit, there is always much to see.

Open: Every day except Christmas Day, Boxing Day and New Year's Day, 10am to 6pm Good Friday - 31 October, 10am to 4pm other times. Adult £8.45, child £4.25. Dogs on leads are allowed.

Opposite: The Italian Garden.
Left: The Rock and Water Garden.

Knoll Gardens

Near Wimborne, BH21 7ND
knollgardens.co.uk

Developed in the 1970s partly on overgrown scrubland, Knoll Gardens now form an oasis of naturalistic beauty, and it is most definitely a place to relax and unwind. The four acres are home to thousands of grasses and flowering perennials from all over the world, although Australasian species are something of a speciality. You are encouraged not to follow a route but to meander along the many paths discovering a number of different gardens and small meadows. At some stage you will reach the Dragon Garden, whose dragon sculpture is a representation of the devil from a legend of St Dunstan, a saint of Wessex and Archbishop of Canterbury. The saint struck the dragon with red hot tongs as he tried to tempt him from his work. Dunstan was the patron saint of goldsmiths and the sculpture is partly in the shape of a harp, the emblem of their trade.

Originally known as Wimborne Botanic Gardens the name was changed to Knoll Gardens in 1988 after Kevin and Sally Martin took over. In 1994 the gardens were bought by Neil Lucas and John and Janet Flude, who brought with them a collection of unusual plants. Neil is now solely responsible for the development of the gardens and is constantly changing and trying out new ideas. An additional side of the enterprise is the Knoll Garden Foundation, a charity set up to refine and promote sustainable, responsible and naturalistic gardening.

Open: 1 February - 23 December, Tuesday to Saturday, 10am to 5pm (4pm November to March). Open Bank Holiday Mondays.
Adult £6.25, under 16 £4.50. Dogs not allowed.

Pictures show the gardens including, far left, the dragon sculpture.

Kingston Maurward Gardens

Near Dorchester off A35, DT2 8PX
kmc.ac.uk/gardens

The seven hundred and fifty acre estate of Kingston Maurward is home to an agricultural college, an animal park and a grade two listed garden. The grand house, a red brick construction, was built between 1717 and 1720 for George Pitt, cousin of Prime Minister William Pitt. He and his wife originally lived in the Elizabethan manor on the estate, which had been acquired by his wife's family from the Maurward family. A succession of Pitts owned the house until 1845, making many additions to the house and gardens. It is said that during one of several visits by George III he admitted his dislike of red brick houses, prompting the owner, William Moreton Pitt, to have the entire house faced with Portland Stone.

In 1845 the house was sold to Francis Martin whose wife taught the young Thomas Hardy who lived at nearby Higher Bockhampton. The house features as Knapwater House in his novel *Desperate Remedies*. Finally, in 1914, Kingston Maurward was bought by the Hanbury family who lived in it until 1939 when it was taken over by the armed forces and used by both the Royal Army Medical Corps and the US Army. After the war Dorset County Council bought the estate and created a Farm Institute, the beginning of the agricultural college we see today. In 1922 the Hanburys had started to develop thirty five acres of formal gardens and these were subsequently restored using old photographs as guides. Today visitors can enjoy these beautiful gardens and relax around the lovely five acre lake.

Open: Daily 3 January - 21 December, 10am to 5:30pm.
Adult £6.50, child £4.50.
No dogs allowed.

Left: The house and gardens.
Opposite: The house from across the lake.

Bennett's Water Gardens

Chickerell near Weymouth, DT3 4AF
bennettswatergardens.com

Several of the delightful gardens in this book have been created from landscapes that were originally anything but scenic and Bennett's Water Gardens are certainly in this category. Situated on the Oxford Clay, a marine deposit from the Jurassic Period, the area once supported a number of brickworks. In 1959 a teacher named Norman Bennett purchased land from the old Putton Brickworks with the idea of growing water lilies in the disused clay pits that had filled with water. The clay was not much use for anything else, but the water lilies thrived. Originally the gardens were a nursery to produce plants for sale, but two further generations of the family have developed the site into the lovely tourist attraction it is today.

The eight acres contain eight small lakes and ponds that hold the National Plant Collection of water lilies and, as home to abundant wildlife, is a registered Site of Nature Conservation Interest. Grassy paths meander around the ponds and there are many beautifully sited seats where you can relax and enjoy the tranquil, picturesque setting. Centrepiece of the gardens is the Monet Bridge, a replica of the Japanese Bridge in Monet's 1899 painting "Water Lily Pond". Many of the original plants bought by Norman Bennett were from the same Bordeaux nursery that supplied Claude Monet for his garden at Giverny.

Open: 25 March - 30 September,
10am to 5pm daily, closed Saturdays.
Adult £8.75, under 16 £4.25.
Dogs not allowed.

Left: Water lilies and one of the ponds.
Opposite: The Monet Bridge.

Forde Abbey

4 miles SE of Chard, Somerset, TA20 4LU
fordeabbey.co.uk

Forde Abbey was once a prosperous Cistercian monastery, supported by 30 000 acres of rich agricultural land. Founded in 1141 and famed as a seat of learning, it thrived for four hundred years until it was handed to the Crown on the Dissolution of the Monasteries under Henry VIII. In 1659 the abbey was bought by Sir Edmund Prideaux, a lawyer and staunch Parliamentarian in the Civil War who afterwards amassed considerable wealth running the postal service for Parliament. He created a fine stately home from the abbey buildings and his descendants, who lived here throughout the eighteenth century, developed the gardens in basically the format we see them today. The early part of the nineteenth century saw a succession of people renting the property, including the philosopher Jeremy Bentham. The abbey and land were sold again in 1863 to Mrs Bertram Evans and through inheritance and marriage finally came to the Roper family

who have cared for it ever since, developing the gardens and house into the magnificent tourist attraction it is today. Many paths lead the visitor through the different parts, to woodland with many fine specimen trees, a rock garden, bog garden and several linked ponds, in one of which is the spectacular Centenary Fountain, at 160 feet the highest powered fountain in England. At the rear of the house is the lovely kitchen garden which, in keeping with the tradition of the old abbey, provides the house and tea room with all their flowers, fruit and vegetables for most of the year. The house is also open to visitors and is a fascinating mix of grand state rooms and austere monastic areas.

Open: Gardens, every day 10am to 5:30pm.
House, 2 April - 31 October, Tuesday to Friday
and Sunday plus Bank Holiday Mondays.
Adult: House and Garden £12.50, garden only £10 (£5
in winter), under 15 free. Dogs welcome in gardens.
Far left: The Centenary Fountain. Left: The kitchen
garden. Pages 37 and 38: The house and gardens.

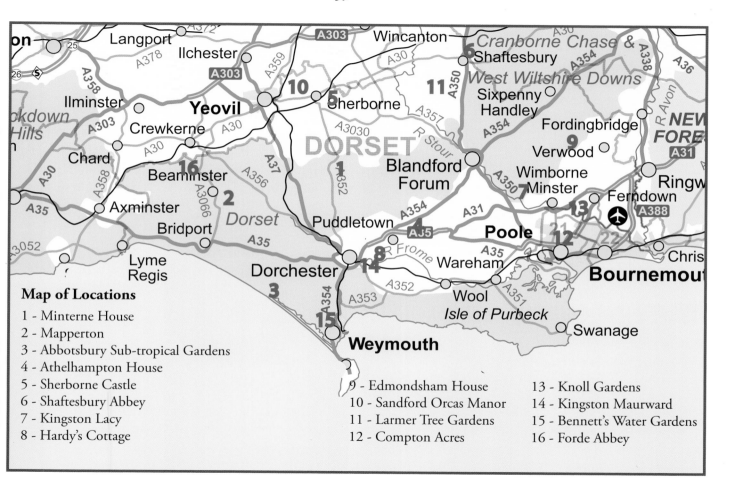

Map of Locations

1 - Minterne House
2 - Mapperton
3 - Abbotsbury Sub-tropical Gardens
4 - Athelhampton House
5 - Sherborne Castle
6 - Shaftesbury Abbey
7 - Kingston Lacy
8 - Hardy's Cottage

9 - Edmondsham House
10 - Sandford Orcas Manor
11 - Larmer Tree Gardens
12 - Compton Acres

13 - Knoll Gardens
14 - Kingston Maurward
15 - Bennett's Water Gardens
16 - Forde Abbey

Acknowledgements

I would like to thank the owners of the wonderful houses and gardens featured in this book, and the National Trust which looks after two of the properties, for allowing me to use photographs I have taken on enjoyable days out. Many have been most encouraging and have commented on and made suggestions to the text.

Notes

The details of opening times and admission prices are correct at the time of writing and several refer to 2016. Please be aware that these may change and check on the website or by telephoning. Many places also offer concessions to students and the elderly, these have not been detailed. Dogs are very welcome in some of the gardens and where they are not allowed, assistance dogs are excepted.

Photographs

All photographs are by the author except on page 2 and far left on page 14, which were kindly supplied by Maria Wingfield-Digby of Sherborne Castle.

Front cover: Forde Abbey
Rear cover: Sherborne Castle